CELTICS LEGENDS ALPHABET

Words by Robin Feiner

A is for 'Red' **A**uerbach. Groundbreaking in every way, Red won 16 NBA championships in 29 years for the Celtics as coach, GM, and president. He drafted the NBA's first African-American player and hired the first African-American coach, all while racking up a whopping 795 regular season wins in Boston—by far a Celtics record!

B is for **B**ill Russell.
The greatest winner in NBA history, Russell amassed 11 NBA championships during his 13-year Celtics career. He's second all-time in the NBA in career rebounds, a five-time MVP, a 12-time All-Star, and considered the greatest defensive player in the history of the sport.
A true Celtics legend!

C is for Bob Cousy.
Although he may look like
your typical Average Joe,
Cousy was anything but.
He introduced several nasty
crossovers, slick moves, and
flashy no-look passes to the
NBA. The Hall of Famer and
Celtics legend led the league
in assists eight times on
his way to six NBA
championships.

D is for **D**oc Rivers. With the hoarsest voice you'll ever hear, Coach Doc demanded excellence and toughness from his Celtics players. He was finally immortalized in Boston lore in 2008 after leading a squad consisting of KG, Paul Pierce, Ray Allen, and Rajon Rondo to a scrappy, well-deserved NBA championship.

**E is for Eddie House.
Though he only played
three seasons for the Celtics,
House was always a solid
contributor off the bench.
His defining moment in white
and green came during the
2008 playoffs, when he
knocked down two clutch
3-pointers to help the Celtics
secure a thrilling Game
4 NBA Finals win.**

F is for Chris Ford.
On October 12th, 1979, Ford scored the NBA's first 3-pointer while donning those flashy clover-green threads. He won an NBA championship alongside Larry Bird two years later, then went on to coach the Celtics for five playoffs-packed years—cementing his status as a Celtics legend.

G is for Kevin **G**arnett. KG proved to Celtics fans everywhere that 'Anything is Possible!' During the 2007–08 season, Garnett helped Boston to a glimmering 66-16 record, was named to the All-NBA First Team, and won Defensive Player of the Year. To cap it off, he punched his Big Ticket by winning the 2008 NBA championship.

H is for John **H**avlicek. 'Hondo' was an instant Celtics legend, winning four NBA championships during his first four seasons. He played 16 immaculate years with the Celtics, tacked on four more NBA titles, and finished as their all-time leading scorer with a mind-boggling 26,395 points.

I is for **I**saiah Thomas. Standing at just 5-foot-9, IT is inarguably one of the toughest pound-for-pound players ever to rock a Celtics jersey. He showcased his incredible grit by dropping 53 points in a Game 2 Playoffs win against the Washington Wizards on May 2nd, 2017—the day of his late sister's birthday.

J is for Dennis **Johnson.**
Starting next to Danny
Ainge in the backcourt,
DJ and his defense helped
propel the Celtics to two
NBA championships. Well-
respected by his NBA peers,
and by Celtics fans, Johnson
eventually had his legendary
No. 3 jersey retired. It now
hangs in the rafters of
Boston's TD Garden.

K is for **K**endrick Perkins. Without 'Big Perk,' the 2007–08 Celtics likely wouldn't have won an NBA championship. This became most clear in 2011 when the Celtics traded their defensive center away right before stumbling to the finish line. For his tenacious play and mean mug, Perk will always be a Boston legend.

L is for Larry 'Legend' Bird. 'The Hick from French Lick,' 'Larry Legend,' 'Kodak'—no Celtics player has more nicknames or legendary moments. As a three-time MVP and NBA Champion, he helped rejuvenate the NBA alongside Magic Johnson in the '80s. Aside from Bill Russell, Bird is the most adored player in Celtics history.

M is for Kevin **M**cHale. With his dazzling array of post moves, McHale was known for putting opponents in an on-court torture chamber. Through his calculated mix of spinning, leaning, jumping, and scoring, 'The Black Hole' played a pivotal role alongside Larry Bird in helping the Celtics capture three NBA championships.

N is for **N**ate 'Tiny' Archibald. While Tiny's Celtics career got off to a rocky start (thanks, ironically, to showing up in Boston overweight), he eventually righted the ship. Celtics fans often remember him for scoring 13 points and dishing out 12 assists in the winning closeout game of the 1981 NBA Finals.

Oo

O is for Shaquille **O**'Neal. While he only played 37 games for the Celtics, 'The Big Aristotle' was certainly beloved in Boston. He provided one last vintage effort to cap a legendary NBA career, dropping 23 points, five rebounds, and five blocks in a win over Charlotte. Celtics fans cheered him on the entire way.

Pp

P is for Paul Pierce.
The 2008 Championship,
trash talking Al Harrington,
countless clutch buckets—
there's no doubting 'The
Truth' has the much-deserved
status of a C's legend. His
greatest moment came in
Game 1 of the 2008 Finals.
Pierce was wheelchaired off
the court due to injury, only
to return and lead Boston
to a triumphant victory.

Q is for **Q**uinn Buckner. Casual NBA fans might forget Buckner, but Celtics fans never will. Known not for his scoring prowess or flashy play but for his hard-nosed defense, Buckner became well-respected by his Celtics peers. In 1984, he won his first and only NBA championship playing along-side Larry Legend.

R is for Robert Parish. Playing for the Celtics alongside Bird and McHale, this 7-foot-1 Celtics legend was a defensive fulcrum equally responsible for making Boston an '80s heavyweight. Of Celtics fans, whom he adored, Parish said: 'I was loved, embraced, and supported. What more can you ask for as an athlete?'

S is for **S**am Jones. Nicknamed 'Mr. Clutch,' Jones cemented his Celtics legacy by coming up time and time again when Boston needed him most. And on a Boston team that won eight consecutive NBA championships from 1961 to 1969, Jones was perhaps their best offensive player aside from John Havlicek.

T is for Jayson **T**atum. Though still young, Tatum has already secured his spot as a Boston legend. On April 30th, 2021, the small, skilled forward dropped a franchise-record 60 points—tying Larry Bird—in a win over the visiting San Antonio Spurs. Perhaps just as loved by Boston fans is Tatum's adorable son, Deuce.

U is for Vitaly 'Ukraine Train' Potapenko. Best remembered for being picked one spot ahead of Kobe Bryant in the 1996 NBA Draft, the Ukraine Train played a stellar, bruising four seasons with the Celtics. Oh, and he might have the greatest nickname in Celtics history—so how could Boston fans ever forget him?

V is for Jan Volk.
While he never graced the court for the Celtics, Volk was key in forming the C's into an NBA powerhouse. During his tenure as General Manager in Boston, the Celtics made it to the NBA Finals three times, capturing one title and losing two to the Los Angeles Lakers.

W is for 'Jo Jo' **W**hite. After a dominant stretch of championships during the '60s, the guys in green were in danger of falling out of relevance. But then along came Jo Jo. The legendary guard averaged over 18 points per game for the Celtics in seven consecutive seasons, winning two NBA champion-ships along the way.

X is for **X**avier 'The X-Man' McDaniel. Known for his rim-rattling dunks and high-flying abilities, the X-Man played with the Celtics for three seasons in the '90s. During the 1992–93 season, McDaniel averaged 13.5 points and six rebounds per game to help lead the Celtics to the playoffs.

Y is for Guerschon **Y**abusele. This French phenom is a Celtics cult legend. Real Boston fans embrace players of his caliber—the gritty, scrappy guys who make the most of their slim playing time. In his debut, Yabusele certainly made an impact, scoring three points and grabbing one rebound in just three minutes of play.

Z is for Larry 'Ziggy' Siegfried. Ziggy's rise to fame is the stuff of legends. Before signing with the Celtics, Siegfried had accepted a job coaching at his former high school. Thankfully, Havlicek convinced him to return to the NBA, where he helped the C's to a string of NBA championships during their dominant '60s run.

The ever-expanding legendary library

EXPLORE THESE LEGENDARY ALPHABETS & MORE AT WWW.ALPHABETLEGENDS.COM

CELTICS LEGENDS ALPHABET
www.alphabetlegends.com

Published by Alphabet Legends Pty Ltd in 2022
Created by Beck Feiner
Copyright © Alphabet Legends Pty Ltd 2022

Printed and bound in China.

9780645487022

ALPHABET LEGENDS